RAINBOW GUITAR

Book 2

HUGH BOYDE

RAINBOW GUITAR BOOK 2

A colourful approach to teaching and learning guitar from the beginning.
For individual or group tuition. Designed for use at Key Stage 2 or 3.

by Hugh Boyde

Illustrations, layout and design by Kate Molloy of 'Little Designs Cambridge' - www.littledc.co.uk

Published by Ringing Strings
33 Impington Lane, Impington,
Cambridge CB24 9LT
UK

www.ringingstringspublications.co.uk

ISBN 978-0-9573503-2-8
2nd edition 2016

Copyright 2014 Hugh Boyde/Ringing Strings. All rights reserved. No part of this publication may be reproduced in any form or by any means – photographic, electronic or mechanical, including photocopying, recording, taping or information storage and retrieval systems – without the prior permission in writing of the publishers.

Section 1: Extending the note range

Look in these boxes to find cross-references to other pages.

To the pupil...

Welcome to Book 2 of Rainbow Guitar!

In Book 1, we learned some simple pieces on strings 2, 3 and 4.

In Book 2, you'll be spreading your wings and playing on all six strings. You'll also be learning to pluck with a mixture of thumb and finger strokes*, and starting to play chords as well as single notes.

Good luck and I hope you enjoy learning these more challenging pieces.

Hugh Boyde

*Or perhaps you are playing with a plectrum? There is some guidance for plectrum players in the Teacher's Notes, which you can download from the website.

Numbering and colouring the strings

In Book 1 you learned to play on the 2nd, 3rd and 4th strings, and each string had a colour.

In Book 2, we will be playing on all six strings. The new strings will be coloured like this:

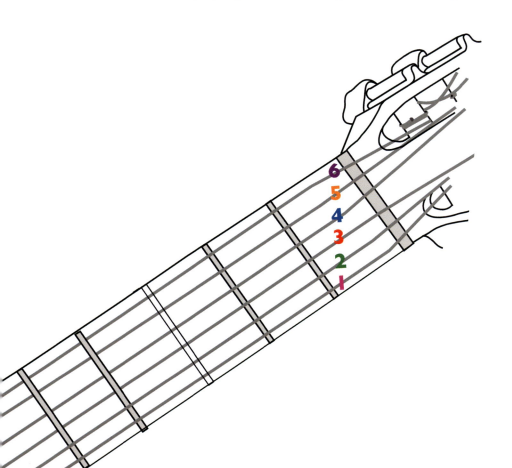

Pink for 1st
Green for 2nd
Red for 3rd
Blue for 4th
Orange for 5th
Purple for 6th

| Complete note reference charts, p30. | | Section 1: Extending the note range | 3 |

Revising the notes from Book 1

A new way of looking at the fingerboard

In this diagram, each stave represents one of the strings of your guitar.
We will be adding to this chart each time we learn new notes in this book.

Use this chart to practise playing and naming all the notes that you know.
Aim to be able to do this at a brisk speed.
Try going from lowest to highest, and from highest to lowest.

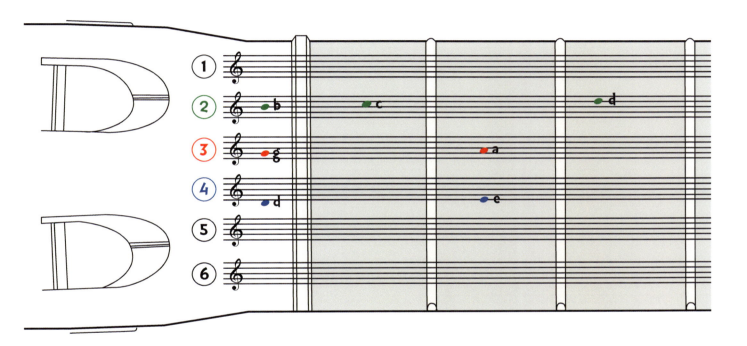

A blank version of this diagram can be downloaded from **www.ringingstringspublications.co.uk**

Section 1: Extending the note range

Chord reference chart p31.

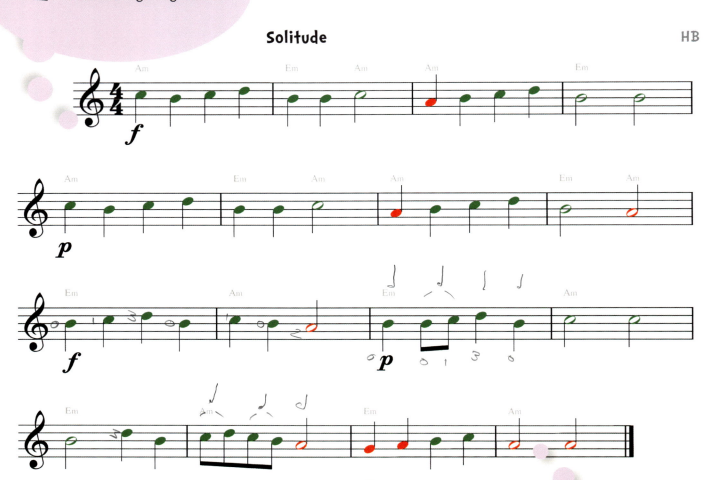

Solitude — HB

DYNAMIC MARKINGS
f = forte = loud
p = piano = quiet
< = crescendo = getting louder

If you want to practise some basic chords as you go through this book, then the CHORD SYMBOLS in grey will help you make up accompaniments to the pieces.

Complete note reference charts, p30.

Section 1: Extending the note range

Two new open strings

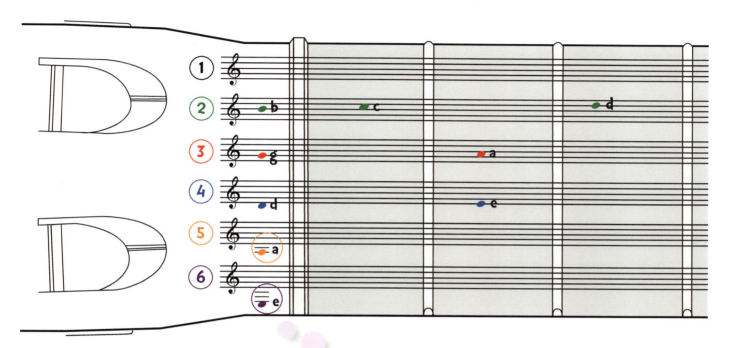

The new notes are very low in pitch, and go below the stave. They are drawn with small extra lines (extensions of the stave) called leger lines.

You can add two new stickers near the bridge of your guitar like this, to remind you of the new strings.

6 Section 1: Extending the note range

Also works with "Good Company", p9.
Extra group parts on website.

Practice with the new notes

Bass part for "Solitude"

HB

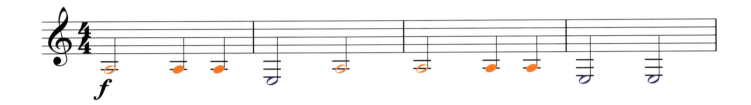

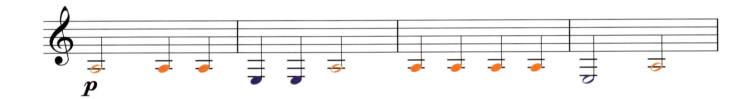

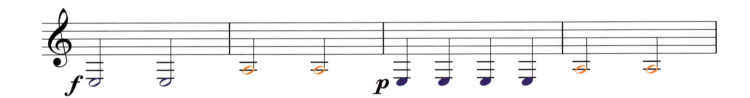

Try the ostinatos with backing track "Endless Journey" from website.

Section 1: Extending the note range

Ostinato (Starting Out)

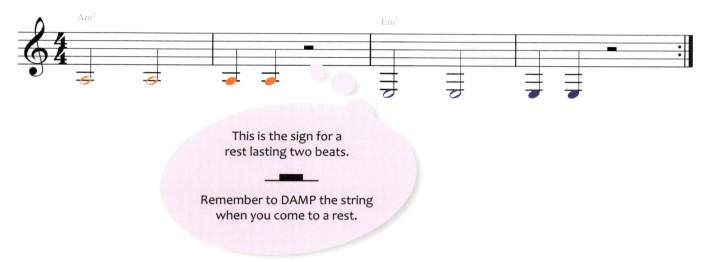

This is the sign for a rest lasting two beats.

Remember to DAMP the string when you come to a rest.

Ostinato (Wheels Rolling)

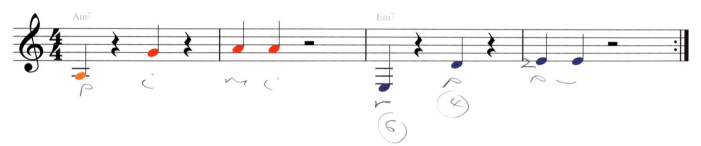

Composing: make up your own ostinato

Can you make up your own ostinato with these notes? See if you can make one which is two bars long.

Then use these notes to play the same ostinato one string lower.

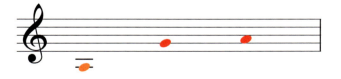

You can write your ostinatos down here if you like.

8 Section 1: Extending the note range

→ Complete note reference charts, p30.

Sharp notes (#)

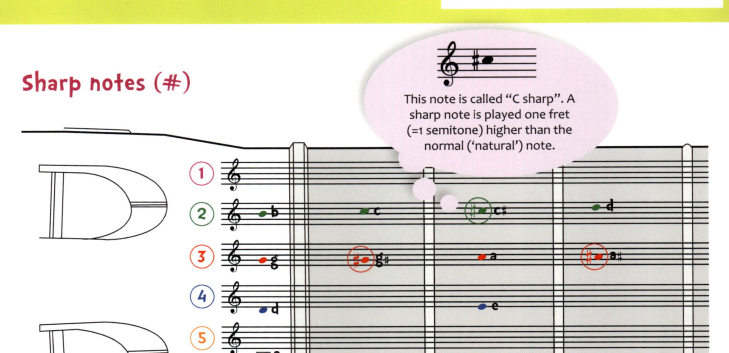

This note is called "C sharp". A sharp note is played one fret (=1 semitone) higher than the normal ('natural') note.

Finger gymnastics

Make mini-scales by playing the notes on the green string slowly up and down, including C#. Then do the same with the notes on the red string.

Name each note as you play, and hold each finger down as you add the next finger.

Practice with sharps

Scale practice with natural notes

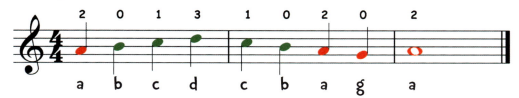

Scale practice with two notes sharpened

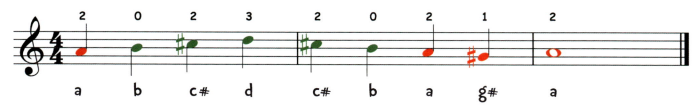

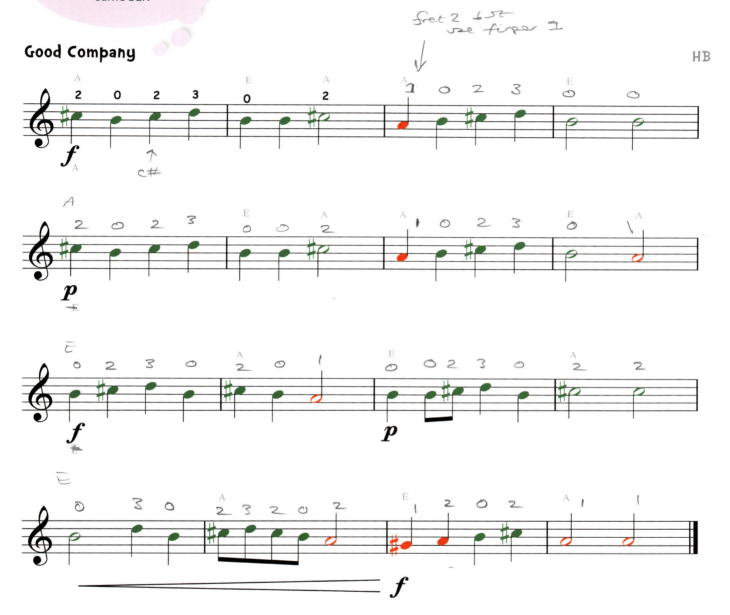

Plucking with "walking fingers"

To begin with, keep your thumb resting on the nearest string (purple) to steady your hand.

Pluck the furthest string (pink) with your index finger. Pluck towards you, in the direction of your elbow.

Now try plucking with the same motion, but using your middle finger. Then try plucking with index and middle fingers in alternation (i + m). This technique is sometimes called "walking fingers" and we will be using it a lot in the next section of the book.

When you look down at your right hand, you should be able to see under your thumb. You should see a triangle shape made by the tip of your thumb, tip of your index finger and the strings.

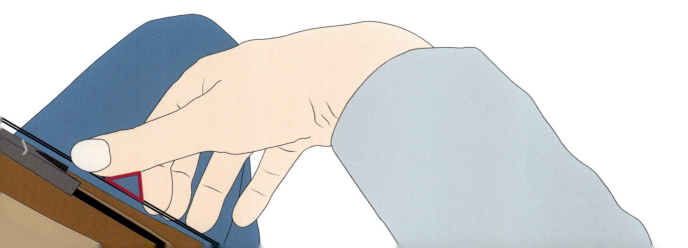

Accompaniment technique p24.
Bass notes p18, p20.

Section 2: Mainly Melody

i = index finger
m = middle finger

Practice with "walking fingers"

Imitating Rhythm

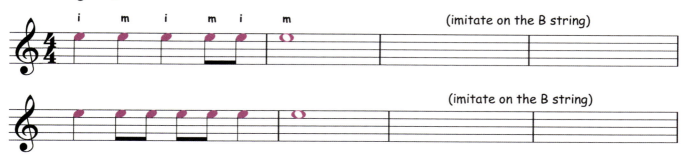

Can you continue this tune by making up more rhythms on the pink string, and then imitating them on green?

Dreamboat

HB

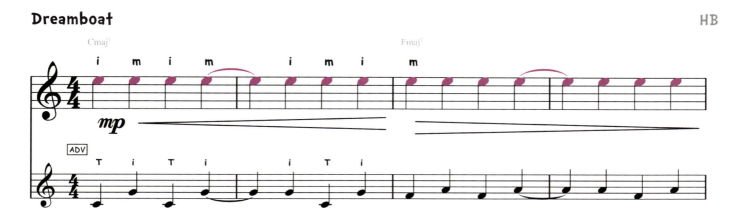

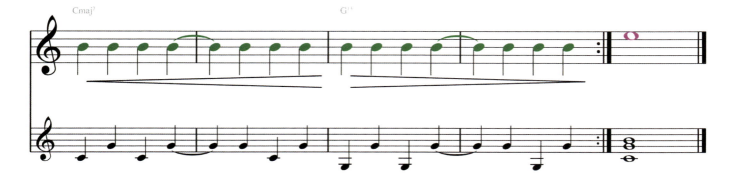

Section 2: Mainly Melody

 Bass notes p18, 20.

After plucking with i and m, use your i finger to damp the string cleanly on the next beat

Two Note Rock

HB

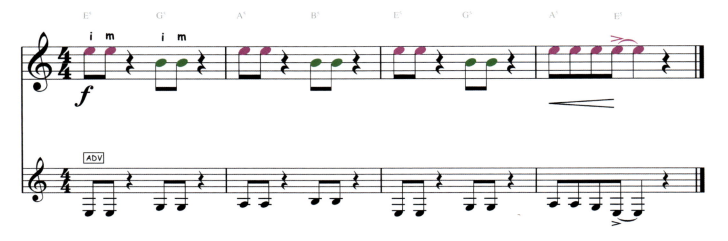

Sailor's Song (open string part)

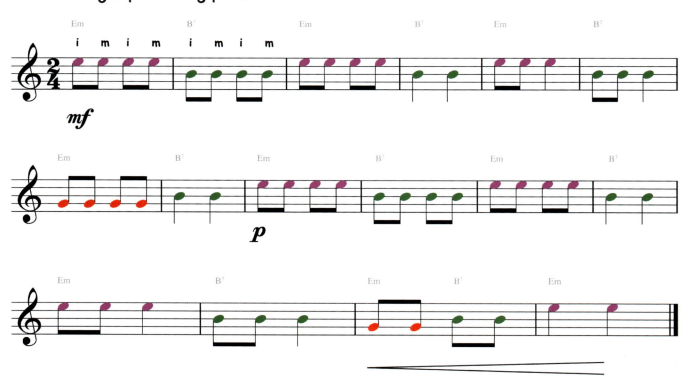

Accompaniment technique p26.
Bass notes p20.

Section 2: Mainly Melody

Fretted notes on string 1

Imitating Melody

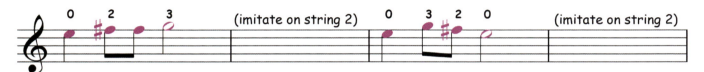

Can you continue this tune by making up more short phrases using E, F# and G, and then imitating them?

Sailor's Song (2nd part)

This can be played by itself or as a duet with the open string part.

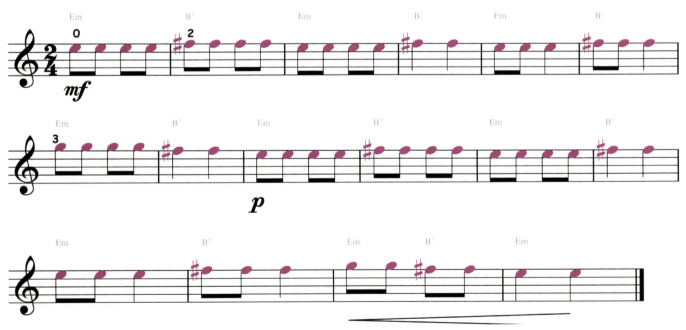

Accompaniment patterns for Sailor's Song

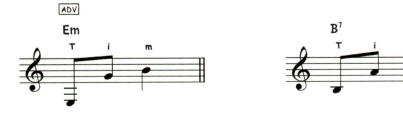

14 Section 2: Mainly Melody

Accompaniment technique p26.
Bass notes p20.

Siren's Call

HB

Accompaniment patterns

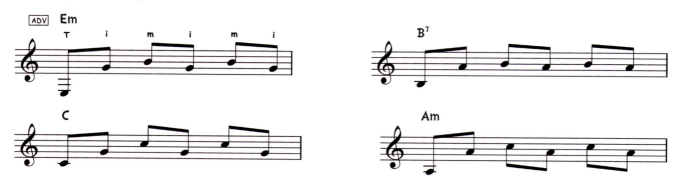

You should be feeling quite comfortable with "walking fingers" by now so why not go back to Book 1 and try some of your old tunes with this new technique?

Accompaniment technique p26.
Bass G note p18.

Section 2: Mainly Melody

15

G major scale

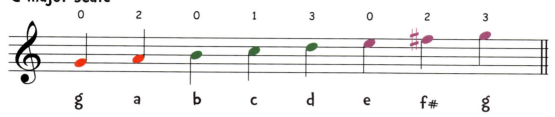

The sharp sign at the beginning of the line is called the KEY SIGNATURE. All notes on this line are to be played sharp.

La Mexicana

HB

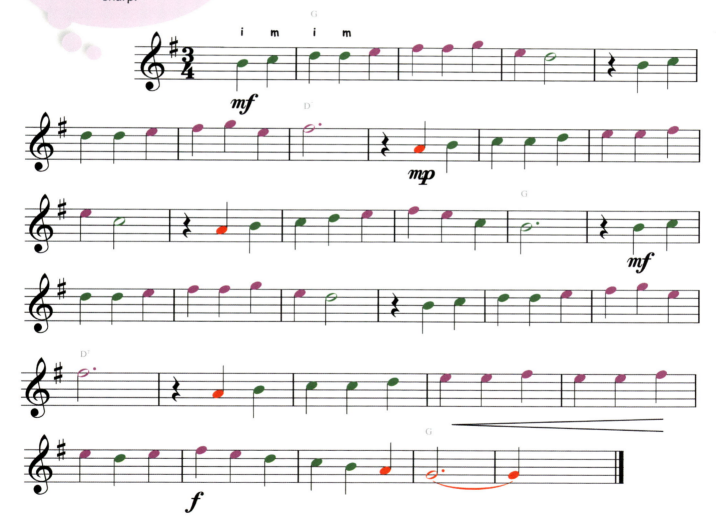

Accompaniment patterns

Section 2: Mainly Melody

Sharps p8. Extended version of Breakdown on website.

Combining thumb and finger plucking

This sign indicates that the notes should be left ringing and allowed to overlap with one another.

sim. = simile = in the same way

The plucking movement should come from the base joint of your fingers and thumb. Aim to keep your wrist steady and relaxed.

Breakdown — HB

Ostinato (Moving on)

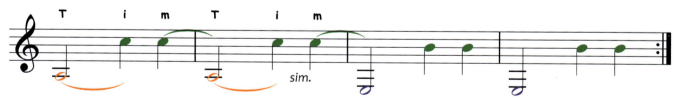

Try playing this pattern along with the backing track "Endless Journey" on the website.

Composition task

Make up some similar ostinato patterns of your own. Use these pairs of notes:

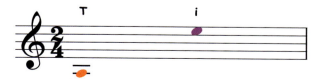 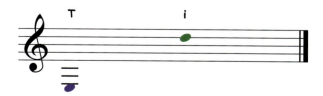

Section 2: Mainly Melody

Complete note reference charts, p30.

Lords and Ladies (solo version)

HB

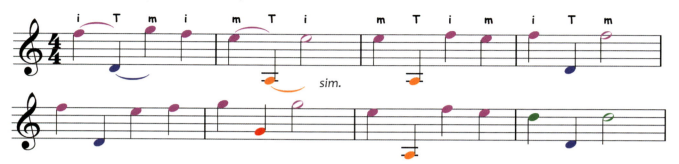

You can play this variation without any accompaniment, or you can play it as an extra part along with the trio version on p17

Fretted notes on string 6

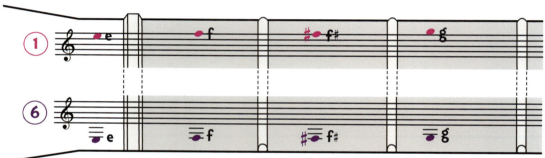

The first and sixth strings have the same name (E). So at each fret on these strings, the note names are the same too.

From Top To Bottom

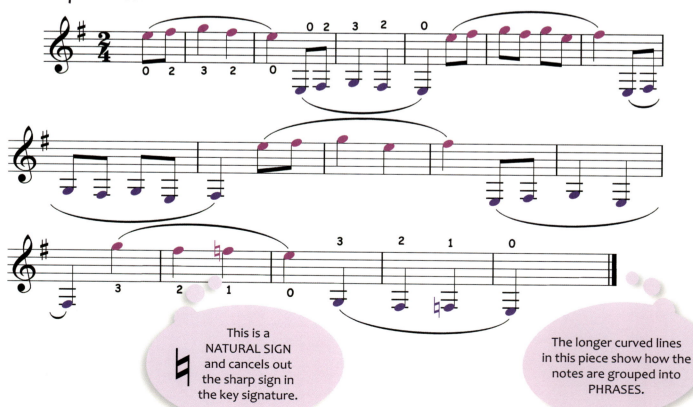

This is a NATURAL SIGN and cancels out the sharp sign in the key signature.

The longer curved lines in this piece show how the notes are grouped into PHRASES.

Section 2: Mainly Melody   19

To help you learn the rhythm, try stamping on the 1 and clapping on the 2 and 3.

Flamenco Flavour
HB

This piece has a very different rhythm! It is based on a rhythm found in Spanish flamenco music. It goes "1-2-3 1-2-3 1-2 1-2 1-2".

X = tap on the face of the guitar. This is called "GOLPE".

◇ This is a HARMONIC note. Instead of pressing the string down on the fingerboard in the usual way, lay your fingertip very lightly on the string just over the 12th fret.

Composition task

Try inventing an unusual rhythm pattern of your own. Then make up a short tune using your rhythm. If you like, you can use a mixture of top and bottom string notes as in "Flamenco Flavour".

Section 2: Mainly Melody

Complete note reference charts, p30.

Fretted notes on string 5

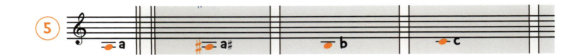

Scale practice

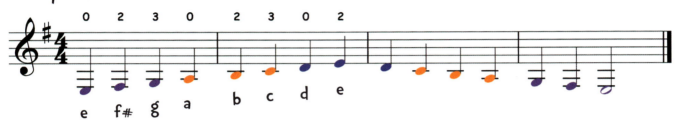

Down Among the Low Notes

Troll Dance

HB

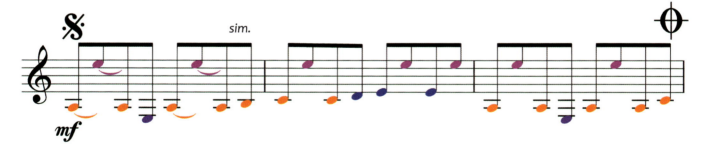

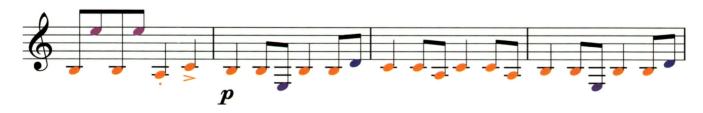

Section 2: Mainly Melody   21

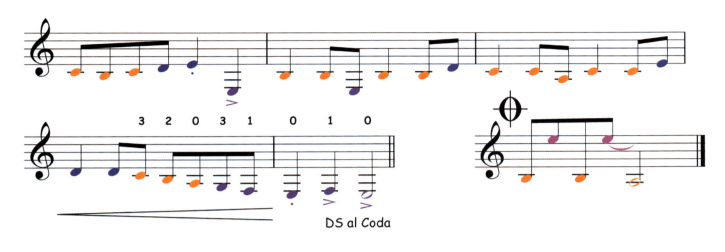

Shifting Ground

HB

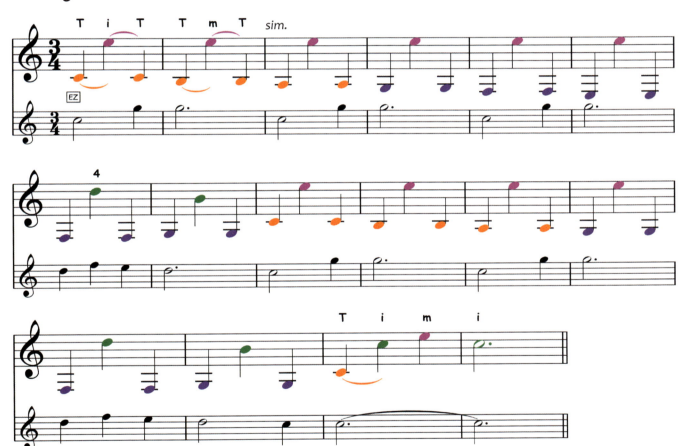

Improvisation practice

Use these notes to improvise freely while your teacher, or another pupil plays Shifting Ground.
Be aware that the key note is C, so this is a good starting and finishing note.

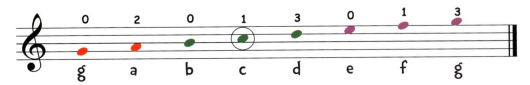

Section 2: Mainly Melody

Complete note reference charts, p30.

Fretted notes on string 4

Scale practice

HB

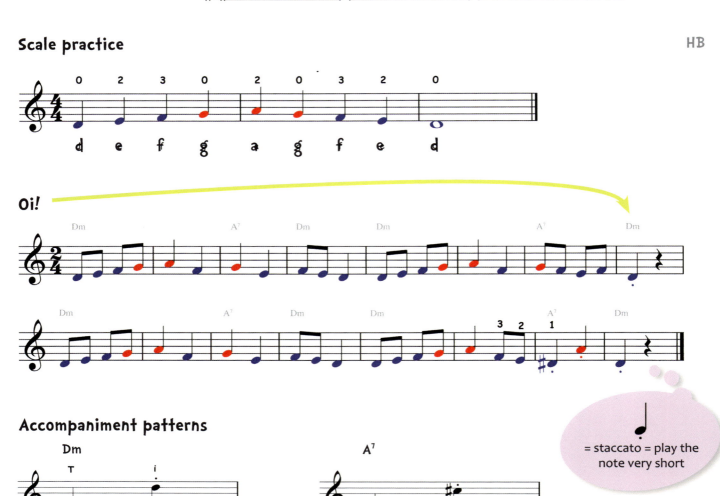

Oi!

Accompaniment patterns

♩. = staccato = play the note very short

Composing with an ostinato

Learn this ostinato and practise it until you can play it smoothly over and over.

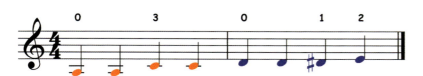

Then try moving the whole finger pattern one string away from you, so you start on string 4 (blue).
Then try the same pattern again starting on string 6 (purple).
Can you make up your own piece by moving the ostinato from string to string?

Chord reference chart p31
Accompaniment technique p26.

Section 2: Mainly Melody   23

Scale practice

HB

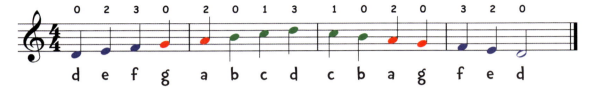

Storm in the Mountains

Accompaniment patterns

Improvisation

Try improvising over the chords of Storm in the Mountains. You can use the notes in the scale at the top of the page.

More plucking patterns (broken chords)

In this section of the book we will be plucking patterns of notes to make chordal acccompaniments: firstly with thumb and index finger (Ti), then adding the middle finger (Tim) and finally the ring finger (Timr). Unused fingers can be left resting on string 1 (pink).

Practice with T and i

You can practise repeating these patterns with the backing track "Endless Journey" (from the website).

Ostinato (Ticking Along)

Ostinato (Winding Road)

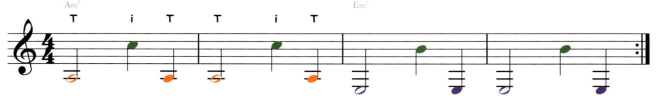

On the following pages, you will often need to alternate between a thumb stroke (down away from you) on a lower string, and a finger stroke (up towards you) on an upper string. You should try to do this without moving the rest of your hand, and this needs very loose and relaxed thumb and finger joints.

Here is a good way to loosen up: try taking a marble or other small round object between your thumb and index finger like this, and twiddle it back and forth. Notice which parts of your hand are moving when you do this.

"Ringing on" sign p16
Bass G note p18.

Section 3: Artful Accompaniment

Floating
HB

Alternative pattern for the G chord (avoiding bottom G)

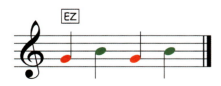

Other ideas for this piece.

1. Ask your teacher to play the melody one octave higher while you play the same accompaniment.

2. Try improvising while someone else plays the accompaniment. You can use the G major scale from p15.

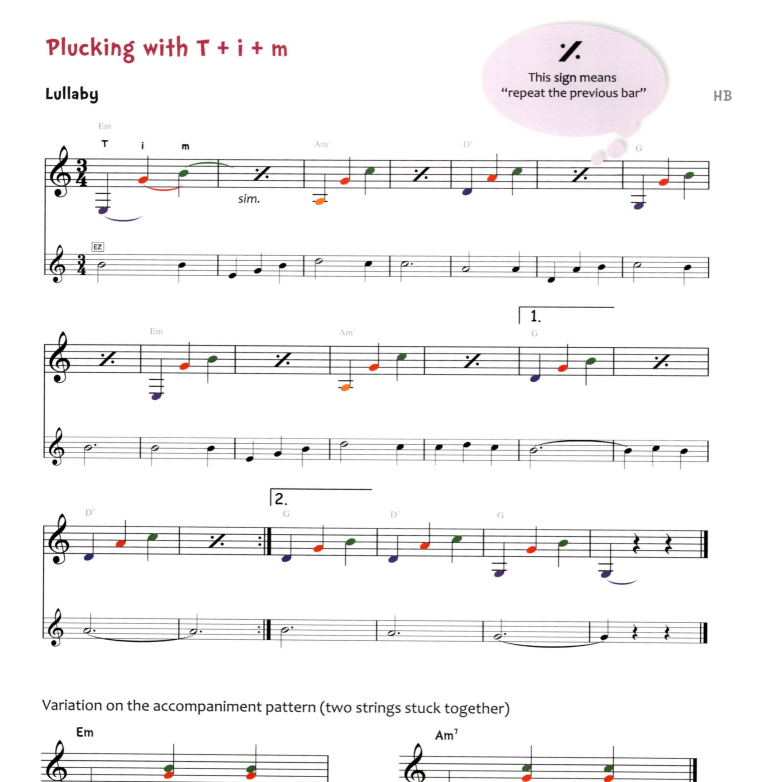

Section 3: Artful Accompaniment 27

Sitting by the Stream

Here is another chordal accompaniment to practise, using T + i + m.
Notice that this one has an irregular rhythm pattern: 123 123 12.

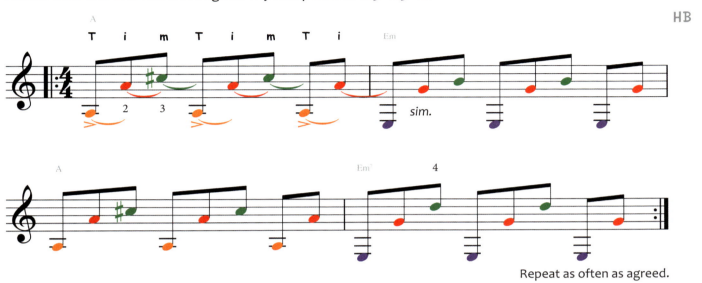

Repeat as often as agreed.

Improvisation

Try improvising your own melody over the accompaniment, using any or all of the notes below.

Composition

Try composing a tune for Sitting by the Stream. You can do this in many ways. Perhaps your improvisation above has already given you some good material? Or you may prefer to start with the opening given below and work out how to continue it.

A possible melody …

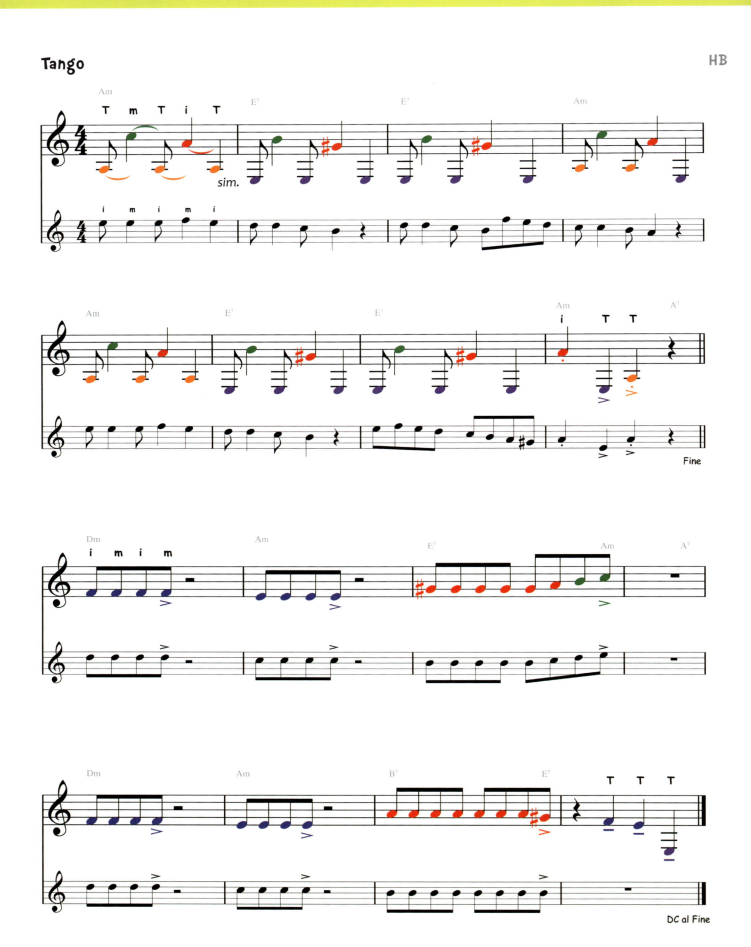

Try accompanying Dreamboat (p11) from the chord symbols, using Timr.

Section 3: Artful Accompaniment

Plucking with T + i + m + r

Ring Finger Blues

HB

Improvisation/Composition

Get someone else to play Ring Finger Blues while you EITHER practice improvising freely over the chords, OR make up a simple riff which can be repeated over the chords (like the one above).
Try using some of the notes below.

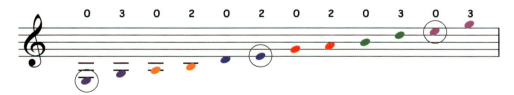

Aim to put together an extended performing version of this piece. You might find the following 4 bars useful as an introduction, interlude, or ending (or all three).

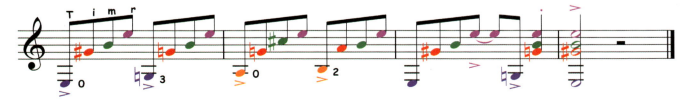

Note reference page

Natural notes up to fret 3

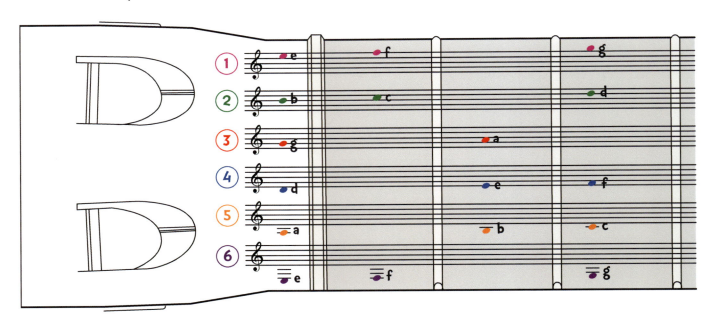

All notes up to fret 3

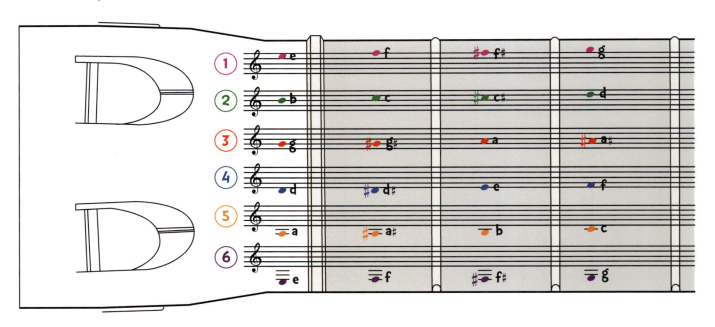

A selection of easy chords on the guitar

These chords can all be used to accompany pieces in this book.

You may find them easy - in which case, you can start to use them straight away to make accompaniments to the pieces in this book. Your teacher will help you make up appropriate strumming or plucking patterns to use.

On the other hand, you may find them hard work to begin with. If so:
- learn just one or two at a time
- only practice them for very short periods of time
- come back to them little and often

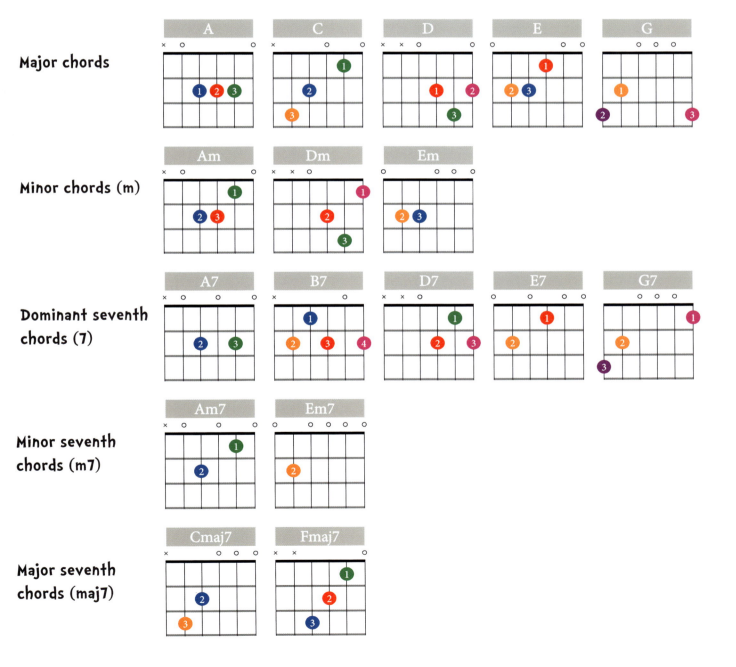